Very Nice Ways to Say
Very Bad Things

Very Nice ways to say Very BAD Things

An Unusual Book of Euphemisms

by

Linda Berdoll

SOURCEBOOKS HYSTERIA™
AN IMPRINT OF SOURCEBOOKS, INC.®
NAPERVILLE, ILLINOIS

Published by Sourcebooks Hysteria, an imprint of Sourcebooks, Inc.
P.O. Box 4410, Naperville, Illinois 60567-4410
(630) 961-3900
Fax: (630) 961-2168
www.sourcebooks.com

Originally published in 2003.

Library of Congress Cataloging-in-Publication Data
Berdoll, Linda
Very Nice Ways to Say Very Bad Things / Linda Berdoll
p. cm.
ISBN-13: 978-1-4022-0885-0
ISBN-10: 1-4022-0885-5
1. English language — Euphemism. 2. English language — Jargon.
3. English language — Terms and phrases. I. Title.
PE1449.B4435 2007
427— dc22
2006100787

Printed and bound in Canada
WC 10 9 8 7 6 5 4 3 2 1

Contents

Gender specific activity, femininity, manhood, manliness, masculinity, sexuality, womanhood, womanliness, intercourse between animate beings, coition, coitus, copulation, fornication, generation, intimacy, lovemaking, magnetism, procreation, relations, reproduction, sensuality, sexuality 73 ☞

Daft, *mentally strange, barmy, unzipped, batty, berserk,*
insane, bonkers, cracked, loony, crazed, cuckoo, demented,
deranged, peculiar, erratic, flaky, fruity, idiotic, insane,
lunatic, mad, maniacal, nuts, potty, psycho, touched,
unbalanced, unglued, unhinged, wacky

Aspersions, brickbats, carping, cavil, censure, denunciation, disparagement, reproach, opprobrium, reproof, stricture, vitriol, epithets, and vituperation

Zounds, I have been bethumped by words.

—*Shakespeare*

Censuring the Inherent Fool: The Lost Art

Few would argue that some behavior is so abhorrent, it demands redressing. Regardless of justification—idiot drivers, impudent clerks, adolescents who have been spawn by the devil—we as a society simply cannot condone smacking the offender upside the head. (Admittedly, we institute this decision partly in deference to decorum, but also in the distinct possibility that said transgressor might be packing heat.) Since throwing the bric-a-brac can become prohibitively expensive, our only alternative is to let fly with a few choice words.

That acknowledged, it is miserably apparent that standards about what is said or heard in public have become remarkably lax. What comes out of the mouths of babes nowadays would have once made a fishwife blush. Not that we deplore vehement notification of character flaws, but chucking stock profanities about does not exhibit the exercise of intellect to which we aspire. To wit:

You stupid, fat fuck

Famous mob boss

or:

𝒴ou show yourself highly fed and lowly taught.

Shakespeare

Granted, no one can hold a verbal candle to Will Shakespeare, but with a few carefully tailored ripostes, one might just leave the miscreants of society flummoxed, if not actually chastened.

Hos and Hounds

Call Him a Rat;
Just Don't Call Him a Mouse.

Once, was one to imply a man less than a
gentleman, one would have to meet him
at dawn accompanied by one's seconds.
The current vogue of anti-heroes
appears to have reversed such a
notion. Calling a man a **rogue,
scoundrel, heel** or even **hump-
ing dog** will not necessarily be
an insult. Therefore, with
honor now discounted, the
male character flaws vulner-
able for attack are intellect,
cuckoldry, wimpiness and
penis size.

> He's a most notable coward, an infinite and
> endless liar, an hourly prose-breaker, the owner
> of no one-good quality.
>
> *Shakespeare*

He is not only dull in himself, but is the cause of dullness in others.

Samuel Foote

Homo-Boobus

To properly vilify the **cabbage-headed oaf,** we must, unfortunately, blaspheme the animal kingdom*—**polecat, skunk, swine, baboon,** (particularly effective with a British inflection) **varmint, goose,** or **donkey.** However, if one calls him a **capon** (a de-knackered chicken), one has hit a triple—not only is he a **graceless lout,** but also a **eunuch**—and unless he was in 4H, unlikely to comprehend the slam.

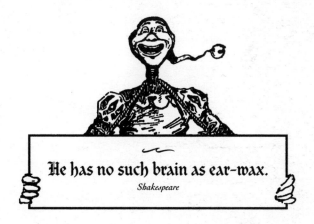

He has no such brain as ear-wax.
Shakespeare

Dullard, dim bulb, dolt, lobberhead, or **flap-doodle** are **inherent fools.** A **lurdane** or **sluggard** is not only a fool, but a lazy fool. The particularly **cantankerous ignoramus** is a **devil child, demon rogue, archfiend, churl, Mephistopheles,** or **carcass fit for dogs.** If one wanted to cover all the

*(In that today few people understand that an ass is actually a four-legged animal, not the gluteal area surrounding one's anus, we omitted it.)

You met your wife's wit

bases, there is *Lusus naturae,* which is Latin for freak of nature. To clarify the subtle difference between a **jerk** and a **dunce,** one must remember not to credit insult that can be more appropriately explained by stupidity.

The Two-timed

Not so very long ago if a man found his wife in bed with another man and took a shotgun to them both, it was ruled justifiable homicide. Hence, it might be wise to make certain there is a clear avenue for escape before one goes rattling this particular cage. If one does have the moxie to do it, there is only one way to go. To quote *Pulp Fiction,* one has to "get medieval on his ass." To do so effectively, one must become intimately familiar with terms as old as the middle ages.

We begin with the word **cuckold,** which many believe originates with the French word for cuckoo bird. This conclusion is apparently due to that dirty bird's penchant for depositing, then abandoning, its monstrous egg into some unsuspecting little wren's nest for it to hatch, then attempt to feed. History has writ **cuckoldry** a shooting offense, giving us to understand quite clearly that men do not want another's cuckoo baby in their nest. In that the cuckoo egg-layer and proprietress of said nest are both female should

going to your neighbor's bed.
Shakespeare

9

throw a monkey wrench in this entire affronted manhood stuff, but as far as we can determine, it has not.

> A man does not look behind the door unless he has stood there himself.
> *Du Bois*

The derivations of most of our terms for cheating appear to be some convolution of the definition for horn—hard protuberance, e.g. penis, and cornu—horn-shaped anatomical characteristic. Indeed, there was a mythical beast called a **bicorn,** which, legend says, used to eat husbands who had unfaithful wives (as to why these victims of infidelity were the ones preyed upon, our crack team of researchers have been unable to ascertain). Then there is the Greek legend of Artemis who caught Actaeon peeking while she was bathing and turned him into a stag, thereupon causing his own hounds to eat him—which maybe served him right.

Hence, the poor cuckold is doomed to suffer, not only his wife's infidelity, but being taunted as a **cornuto** or **buck's face** (has horns, you know), **suffering the forked plague, prey to the bicorn,** or, get this, **wearing Vulcan's badge:**

> The roof of Vulcan, her, by many a gift
> Seduced, Mars won, and with adult'rous lust
> The bed dishonour'd of the King of fire.
>
> *Cowper — The Odyssey of Homer*

One must concede that in issuing the jibe, Vulcan's badge, it could be misconstrued. A certain element of the population may not understand that in this context, Vulcan pertains to the God of Fire and has nothing whatsoever to do with Star Trek.

A **wittol** is aware he is being cheated on and puts up with it (what was Camilla Parker Bowles' husband's name anyway?). If he is aware and enraged, he is **horn-mad.** If he is cheating on her, she is a **cuckquean** and usually **The Last to Know.** If the correspondent in this affair is a man, he is, indeed, **Actaeon.** His female counterpart is an inconstant, faithless sore in the side of a man and, no doubt, a wanton hussy. The entire activity is, quite aptly, named **cornucopia** —horn of plenty (we suppose, because there is plenty of horniness going on).

ATTENTION: It is imperative that when one inflicts any of the above abuse, it must be done with extreme superciliousness, else its just not gonna work.

11

The Invertebrate

In cockfighting, a white tail feather among the plumage of a gamecock denotes inferior breeding and therefore a less combative rooster. When calling a person's courage into question, the accusation of **showing a white feather** may now seem a bit obscure, but for centuries, it was tantamount to saying **"what a candy-ass."**

In common parlance a **cur** is a mongrel dog, but its second definition dating also from the thirteenth century, is coward. From the Middle Ages comes **recreant,** which as an adjective describes a begging of mercy (we understand not an uncommon occurrence during those times) and by token, one who does so, a coward.* In the first half of the 18th century, **funk** meant "a state of paralyzing fear," hence one who funks is, too, a coward. As to how and why this term was usurped by the music industry in the '70s remains a mystery, but it will arbitrarily remove the word funky from possible cowardly insults.

*If faced with being drawn and quartered we are not certain who among us would not go down screaming like a **woman bringing forth child.**

He led his regiment from behind, He found it less exciting.
W.S. Gilbert

> Cowardice is distinguished from panic by the inability to suspend the imagination.

Therefore, the terms that imply the lack of stalwartness of someone's innards are: **lily-livered, yellow-bellied, spineless, faint,** or **chicken-hearted, pantywaist,** or a **gutless wonder.** One might avoid **wimp** and **big baby**—they lack imagination. Woody Allen says he is not a hypochondriac, but an **alarmist.** That makes our list, as does **milquetoast, caitiff, craven, dastard,** or **poltroon.** Save **sissy-britches** or **wienie** for when one has to pull out the big artillery.

☞**FYI:** We note a rectal sub-category as it relates to the frightened. First, there is the **pucker factor,** which refers to the degree of fear that causes one's sphincter to tighten. Contrarily is the green heron or **shitepoke** which, when startled into flight, defecates. It goes without saying that whatever category one may find oneself in when, say, one's aircraft plummets or the IRS makes inquiries, should remain between oneself and one's laundress.

He Who Is Not Nick-Named Tripod

There was an old man named Ringer,
Who was seducing a beautiful singer.
He said with a grin,
"Now, I've got it in."
Said she, "You mean that's not your finger?"

14

Of the euphemisms we uncovered for a man **less favored by nature (hung like a chicken, pencil-dick and bug-fucker),** we can only recommend **under-endowed** and **three-inch fool,** so this entry will be blessedly small (no pun intended).

The Five-Letter Woman

She was a woman of mean understanding,
Little information and uncertain temper.
Jane Austen

Historically the most effective means to rebuke any woman was to disparage her virtue (that or possibly her fashion sense). Nowadays, **un-virtuous** and **unladylike** are probably as useless as insults go as **un-gentlemanly.** Yet however ubiquitous its use, we can agree that calling a disreputable female a **bitch** (or even **puppy's mama**) is not only common, but an insult to female dogs. **Harpy, harridan, slattern,** or **shrew** may be vintage, but they are just pithy enough for general reproach of shrill, hateful behavior. When faced with an irredeemably cantankerous woman, she may well be the **Devil's Sister.** (If she appears to find this in any way complimentary, a keen sense of self preservation might suggest one **run like a cheap pair of pantyhose.**)

Foul Sluts

Even if the **succubus** that one's brother intends to marry is a **fornicatress** that has **seen more pricks than a dartboard,** we encourage one not to refer to her as a **slut, tramp, hussy, trollop, round-heeled floozy,** or **dirty-legged Jezebel.** One might get away with **"she's been around the block more times than the Good Humor man"** to others, but unless he actually asks your opinion, one might do well to refrain from comment at all.

Other analogies for that woman who has been **laid on every flat rock in three counties** include the **town pump** or any noun that can

be ridden: **bicycle, hobby horse, barber's chair, ferry, hackney, taxi,** etc. A **badger** is a loose woman who is particularly ill-scented.

Disclaimer: This information is offered only for elucidative purposes.

☞**FYI:** If one believes that a woman is **of accommodating morals** and decides to say so publicly, one has **bewhored** her (or, depending on one's 'hood, possibly beho-ed her). Be certain that she doesn't mind the advertisement or have your affairs in order, for it is said: "Hell hath no fury like pussy with a pistol."

Y'wanna piece of me, sweetie?

Dog City

If while mentally cruising some parallel universe, one believes it a good idea to slander a masculine woman, at least have the good sense to avoid calling her a **diesel-dyke** or **hell pig. Virago, beldame, trolleymog, daggletail,** or **buffarilla** mean precisely the same thing and their relative obscurity may offer one just enough time to elude being beaten to a pulp.

NOTE: We have been told that if one is in a Spanish-speaking country, it is also advisable not to compliment a strong woman by calling her **macha.**

At a loss for words, hockey puck? Quote Shakespeare.

BULLETIN: The unparalleled king of insults is not Don Rickles.

As has certainly not passed one's notice, Shakespeare marshals up gems of abuse that would whoosh right over the average boor's head. Therefore, appropriating The Bard's words to one's own needs will serve a dual purpose. It confounds the ignorant and catches the erudite off guard. Hence:

Shakespeare, Addressing Individual Mounds of Foul, Undigested Lumps of Donkey Entrails:

FOR THOSE OF THE FEMALE PERSUASION

Hag of hell, fat chuff, latten bilbo (brass shackles), painted maypole, long-tongued babbling gossip, and Amazonian trull.

FOR MEN WHO HAVE FALLEN OUT OF ONE'S FAVOR

False hound, untutored churl, rank weed, insolent cracker, unlettered small-knowing soul, odoriferous stench, pigeon-egg of discretion, dilatory sloth, homely swain, clod of wayward marl, dunghill groom, puke-stocking, improvident flea, ronyon (mangy or scabby creature), roastmeat for worms, princox (fop), cacoethes (one with insatiable desire, usually disreputable), mad mustachio'd purple-hued maltworm, prick-eared cur of—(fill in the name of town, school, or neighborhood the cur claims as home), and whoreson.

FOR ONE'S BOSS

Old feeble carrion, scolding crookbank, embossed carbuncle, white-livered-red-faced prince of fiends, cacodemon (evil spirit), maggot pie, execrable wretch, beef-witted, or sodden-witted implorer of unholy suits.

TO VERBALLY BACKHAND GROUP OBNOXIOUSNESS

You rabble of vile confederates, herd of boils and plagues, petty spirits of region low, strangely visited people, foul and pestilent congregation of vapors, college of witcrackers, dissolute crew, or base lackey peasants.

Under certain circumstances, profanity provides a relief denied even to prayer.

Mark Twain

Sacre Bleu: Profanities and Expletives

The "F" ing Word & Other Intensives

Veritable, sure enough, or **bona-fide** are perfectly respectable intensifiers when one needs, well, emphasis. Unfortunately, **fucking** seems to be the hands-down pejorative of choice in modern society. This being the case, we believe a little historical perspective couldn't hurt . . .

No matter how many people believe it true, it is highly unlikely that the word "fuck" is an acronym of **For Unlawful Carnal Knowledge** or that other old chestnut, **Fornicate Under Consent of the King.** Eric Partridge believed it evolved from the German word ficken for "to strike." Like most, he found the word objectionable. He, however, categorized it along with words that he considered sadistic representations of the male's part in copulation: **clap, strike, thump, nail,** and, yes, **bang.** Webster's offers the derivations, *fokken* (Dutch, to breed) or *fokka* (Swedish, to copulate). Others suggest the French word ***foutre,*** to thrust, and even *firk* (English 1600's), to beat or to lash. However it originated, it has been in use and considered a vulgarity the better part of a millennium. As an intensive, Webster's calls it meaningless. There are those who would disagree.

To avoid inciting an affronted swoon by the more sensitive souls of society, acronyms have been embraced in place of a number of phrases that include the "f" word. Specifically, we have **GFY,** which instructs one to do something anatomically impossible (Go Fuck Yourself); **GFU,** a moron (General Fuck-Up); and **NFW,** an implausibility (No Fucking Way). Related acronyms include **SNAFU,** a cynical expectation of any situation in which the military is involved (Situation Normal, All Fucked-Up); **FUBAR,** unrecognizably mussed (Fucked-Up Beyond All Recognition); and there is the sarcastic **BFD** (Big Fucking Deal).

Additionally, when one has been indisputably wronged, one has been **RF**—Royally Fucked (also known as the **king's elevator**—**the royal shaft**). Just for the record, a **flying fuck is what one does not give**, not airborne copulation. And **abso-fucking-lutely** means beyond a shadow of a doubt.

Merde

The four-letter word for defecation has been in use for eons —which allows that antiquity does not necessarily dictate grand lexicon. It is possible to avoid the vulgarity of the word **shit** completely, as **feces, manure,** and **dung** all mean the same thing. (Small point of interest: feces refer to human waste, manure and dung, animal.) Other selections tend to be polysyllabic but are colorful—**meadow dressing, bovine excrement, horse apples, corral confetti,** etc. Granted, if one is discussing political matters, it may be impossible to avoid using (or even shouting) **bullshit.** However, if one does not want to compromise decorum completely, that can be shortened to **B.S.** Or, call it **hogwash, heifer dust,** or **lip-gloss. Bull-chips** might do in a pinch but, in all probability, not what pops out of one's mouth when faced with ultimate doom (at which time one will most likely be **up Shit Creek**). Indeed, sources report that when the black boxes are recovered from airplane crash sites, invariably the last words on the tape are "Uh-oh," "Fuck!" and "Oh, shit. "

Of course, one can use the French, **merde** or speak of **"a short French expletive"** which would in fact allow one to perform a rather impressive circumlocutory hat trick, a euphemism for a euphemism for euphemism.

When one finds it necessary to point out the limitations of another's character via the

alimentary canal, it is our position that it is preferable to
enlist mock Latin such as *excrementum cerebellum vincit*
rather than call someone a **shit-head**.

Other expressions that would benefit such translation are:
shit list (a mental note of **personae non gratae**); the **shitty
end of the stick** (the bad end of a bargain — often known
as **the shaft**); to **shit or get off the pot** (or **fish or cut bait**).
To **shit in high cotton** is to have attained a higher standard
of living. But **not knowing shit from Shinola**—well, that
means . . . owing to stupidity one cannot tell feces from
shoe polish. Someone whose continued presence is an

annoyance **sticks like shit to a shovel.** Alternatively,
shit on wheels reflects an over-inflated opinion of oneself.
(We, however, could in no way determine how one could
deign this to be a self-compliment).

Shit a brick technically means discharging a copious and
compacted bowel movement, but colloquially it refers to
accomplishing the impossible. Lastly, to be so angry as to
perform said impossibility is engaging in a **shit-fit** (also
known as **pitching a bitch**). Certainly there are Latin
instructors standing by to assist us.

Vexed

As ancient a word as is **piss,** it was not until the last century that humankind found use for it beyond the single
verb or noun. Nowadays, if one is **pissed off,** one is actually **choleric** (and undoubtedly with one's **panties in
a bunch** or **knickers in a knot**). Shakespeare expressed
it thusly: "𝔜𝔬𝔲 𝔡𝔬 𝔪𝔢 𝔱𝔥𝔢 𝔪𝔬𝔰𝔱 𝔦𝔫𝔰𝔲𝔭𝔭𝔬𝔯𝔱𝔞𝔟𝔩𝔢 𝔳𝔢𝔵𝔞𝔱𝔦𝔬𝔫."

Other urinary-based euphemisms and their more civilized
translations: **full of piss and vinegar** (effervescent), **piss
away** (squander the inheritance — leaving oneself **without a
pot to piss in**), and **piss blood** (work with extreme diligence).
A **piss-ass** is a worthless individual (occasionally called an
arseworm), to engage in a **pissing match** is an endeavor
that is certain to be unproductive, and if one is **piss-poor,**
one is monetarily disadvantaged (e.g., without cable).

Piss ugly is extremely un-
attractive and if **piss-faced,** one
is overly medicated by alcohol.

The heretofore unheard of, **pissed as
a newt** has come to our attention. As we
have not personally been confronted by an
outraged salamander, we are uncertain of the
etymology or history of this term. We can only
labor under the supposition that in this situation,
"pissed" does mean vexed, for we believe one even less
likely to come across a drunken newt than a mean one.

☞ NOTE: The colorful late U. S. Vice President, John
Nance Garner is oft quoted as saying the office of Vice
President was not worth a bucket of warm spit. Those who
knew the man insist he didn't use the word, "spit."

Oaths and General Vituperation

If a potty mouth forsakes stock curses and lets fly with the likes of **Jumpin' Jehosaphat,** just imagine the stunned silence. Likewise, **pshaw, Land a Goshen, Lord love a duck, criminey, Ye Gods and little Fishes, pish-tosh, My**

Great Aunt Gussie — or as Great Aunt Gussie might say, **hells bells and panther tracks!** While we understand these oaths are insufficiently obscene for some, calling someone a **pinhead** instead of a **fuck-head** will neither get one ticketed nor **beat like a one-legged step-child.**

The Abode of the Wicked Dead

Down, down to hell; and say I sent thee thither

Shakespeare

Technically **hell** is the nether realm of the devil in which the damned suffer everlasting punishment. In other words, a real **sticky wicket.** The word in and of itself is not naughty. Nevertheless, everyone knows (or at least suspects) that damning someone to it is considered a blasphemy.

Hence, it is not surprising that an entire cottage industry of euphemistic splendor has erupted from that word's roots. Indeed, the lengths to which people go to say it without "saying it" is quite remarkable: **Hades, Hail Columbia, blue blazes, Cain, tarnation, Sam Hill, Kingdom Come, You Know Where,** or any place that implies **"down there,"** the **hot place, netherworld, lower regions,** etc. Although the Victorians gave us **heck, perdition** has been a suitable alternative since the 14th century. Today we seldom hear the once popular **Go to Helen B. Happy.** A shame, really.

Hellacious is a multi-purpose adjective that can mean either: exceptionally powerful, remarkably good, extremely difficult or extraordinarily large. To be **hell-bent** is recklessly determined come **hell or high water.**

Doggone and Up Yours

Oh darn, dang, confound, consarn, dagnab, dash, blank, or **blast** followed by **it,** are all euphemistic replacements for the word, **damn.** All denounce someone or something as evil. Truly genteel society frowns on these seemingly benign adjectives as well as **bloody, bleeding, blamed, all-fired, dad-gummed, dratted,** and **cotton-picking.**

At one time, a curse was serious business. No one took lightly being consigned by another to hell, which may be why **Go to the Devil** morphed into **Kiss My Ass. Go jump in the lake** or **take a long walk off a short pier** are only nicer sounding ways to tell someone to **fold it five ways and shove it where the sun don't shine.**

Silent Disparagement (The Bird and His Friends)

Although many think of it as contemporary, *digitus infamis* or *digitus impudicus* (infamous or indecent finger) as a phallic symbol has been referenced in literary works as early as ancient Rome. **Mad-as-a-hatter** Caligula was rumored to hold up his middle finger for supplicants to kiss.

There is the obvious suggestion of genitalia in fist and extended middle finger, but we have heard that during early warfare, captured enemy archers had their fingers removed so they couldn't draw a bow. Therefore, holding up two fingers (index and middle) backwards to one's enemy signified one could still do them damage. One could premise that's pretty much saying "f--- you."

From the fight scene in Romeo & Juliet, which commenced with the snapping of thumbnail under the front teeth, to Texas A&M's upraised "Gig 'Em

Aggies" thumb, we see the ultimate insult can be insinuated by other than extended middle finger. In the Arab world, palm down, middle finger waggling downward means the same as raised middle finger in the West.

FYI: The little finger offered as suggestion of a, shall we say, modestly proportioned male part is not of modern origin. Seek ye the Bible. I Kings 12:10.

To express general disrespect, there is the **Cock a Snook,** also known as **Ann's Fan** or **Pulling Bacon,** which is the thumb on nose, fingers waving. To grasp one elbow and

 raise a fist is one of the commonest insult found worldwide, but is not universal. That title must go to displaying one's naked backside. Anthropologists say mooning predates *Braveheart* and, loosely translated, meant "eat shit."

After the fall of Bagdad, we saw Iraqis beating the tar out of portraits and statues of Saddam Hussein with their shoes, revealing to westerners one of the strongest insults of their culture — that of sticking the sole of your shoe in someone's face.

As there are any number of variations of armpit, bicep, fist, finger, thumb, nose, crotch and spit . . . maneuvers to express disrespect in different cultures, if one must hail a cab, say, in Greece or New York, do so with all due caution.

Circumlocution

Because we often toss them about willy-nilly, we may forget that euphemisms serve a greater purpose than merely keeping the ladies at a garden party from glaring at us over the top of their spectacles. A glib turn of phrase can spare wounded feelings, a few mincing words keep lawyers at bay.

Until the Victorian era, however, the euphemistic mother lode had not really begun to be mined. Once Queen Victoria was on her throne and her minions on high alert, there was little that couldn't be accused of having a sexual, and therefore, evil, connotation. Everything had to be renamed. Hence, a bull became a **cow's spouse** and one's buttocks, **sit-upons.** One can only imagine how dicey it must have been sitting down at Sunday dinner for some poor soul trying to ask for a specific piece of chicken.

A Woman of Expansive Sensibilities

Paphos was an ancient city of Cypress known for worshipping Aphrodite. The well-traveled, or at least well-read,

Victorian men found it quite sly to call a prostitute or her doings, **Paphian.** Further 19th century circumlocution favored **demimondaine, academician, abbess, courtesan,** *Fille de jolie* (fun gal) or ***nymph du pave*** (streetwalker). The term of choice for those whose professions or predilections sought to save her soul: she was a **fallen woman.**

One rarely hears of a **lady of certain description** or **painted woman** anymore, but one would have to be pretty obtuse not to understand the meaning. A little more recent is **woman of the night, streetwalker, naughty girl,** and **commercial sex worker.** A quick check of our Yellow Pages did not uncover services by **call girls.** However, **escort, model,** and **actress** listings are numerous and offer "discreet billing."

As for the specific establishment where these shenanigans take place, a century ago it was referred to as a **leaping academy, vaulting school, disorderly house, knocking**

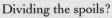

Dividing the spoils?

shop, or **chamber of commerce.** However dated that sounds, one must agree that today's **snake ranch** or **slut hut** is not much of an improvement. Granted, **whorehouse** is to the point, but just a tad crude. If compelled to speak of it, polite society might say it is a **brothel, place of accommodation, bagnio,** or **seraglio.** Or, depending on your frame of mind, **house of ill-repute.**

Furthering the subject, we proffer that he who pimps prostitutes is not a **pussy peddler, hole-toller, buttock broker, vent renter,** or **crack salesman,** but a **panderer, procurer,** or the French, *souteneur,* and with or without **pimp-mobile,** undoubtedly, a **louse** (editorially speaking).

For he who thinks he is pulling the wool over by describing she who is gyrating upon his lap as an **exotic dancer** rather than a **stripper,** be advised, he can go one step further in self- (or wife) delusion. Employing the term **ecdysiast** is even more oblique. Although ecdysis does sound like a moderately uncomfortable medical procedure, it is actually the molting or shedding of a skin like a snake.

Men Much Taken With Wenching

As **lechery** appears to be an accepted major by college-age males, modern vernacular has responded. Nowadays, he who pursues such activities with undue vigor is a **walking hard-on.** If the little **stud muffin** has **seen more tail than a toilet seat,** when the dean writes home of his expulsion, he may be described as **of distempered blood** and **duteous to vices.** (Well, maybe if he was at Oxford.)

We can call him a **debaucher, libertine, flesh-monger, incubus, Lothario, insatiate,** or *roué,* but it doesn't make him any less irredeemable. Of course, if he insists he is a man of the world by way of visiting **three county fairs and a goat-fucking,** he undoubtedly is a *bon viveur.*

The Prevaricator

Liar, Liar, Pants on Fire

At one time, to question a person's honesty was no trivial matter. Such was its consequence; one dare not bandy the word *liar* about. Therefore, the more innocent **prevaricator** was often accused of only **spinning a windy** or **embroidering the truth.** A **mountebank** would **lie like a rug,** and a **charlatan was crooked as a barrel of snakes. To piss in someone's pocket** means one is feeding him a pack of lies.

Honest Bob's Used Wagons

If you seek the finest for the least, Honest Bob can procure it for you.

> A lie can travel halfway around the world
> while the truth is putting on its shoes.
>
> *Mark Twain*

denunciation, disparagement, reproach, opprobr

37

It's hard to believe that a man is telling the truth
when you know that you would lie
if you were in his place.

H.L. Mencken

Current euphemisms such as **terminological inexactitude** and **economy with the truth** dilly-dally about. When last we checked, thou shalt not bear false witness against one's neighbor was still the ninth commandment. So **"I misspoke"** won't cut it with the keeper of the pearly gates.

> A lie is an abomination to the Lord
> and a very present help in trouble.
> *Adlai Stevenson*

Although not technically lying, **pettifoggery** fits into this category for general unscrupulousness. Since the 16th century, it has described the antics of two or more lawyers haggling unceasingly about minute matters thereby inflating their client's bill—thus proving the old axiom about the more things change, the more they stay the same.

Q. Why do lawyers wear neckties?

A. To keep the foreskin from crawling up their chins.

Tuft Hunters and Suck-ups

In English colleges such as Oxford, the aristocrats wore special tassels (tufts) on their mortarboard hats to denote their status. The more **obsequious** among the student body sought them out, ergo—**tuft-hunters.** To most, these truly annoying **suck-ups** are **sycophants.**

If overtaken by an undeniable need to publicly decry this character flaw, one might whip out one's French dictionary and sniff *"leche-cul"* (butt-kisser) right in the **servile flatterer's** face. Once out of high school, however, it is advisable to sling more derogatory comments such as **bootlicker** and **brown-noser** behind the back. If you do cast this particular stone, understand that bootlicker is associated with the habit of kissing the feet of kings and therefore conveys a modicum of respectability (only barely). However, it is often overlooked that **brown-noser** refers to the result of smooching another part of the anatomy. Shakespeare called them all puling pickthanks.

In the Altogether

By definition, if one finds oneself *in disbabille,* one is care-lessly attired. In truth, that French term is often nothing less than an outright accusation of misconduct. Not only has one been cited for having one's clothes in a muss, but also by having them become that way because one has been fooling around. Standard advice: Gather whatever dignity one is able to muster, deny everything and make a brisk exit.

Clothes make the man. Naked people have little or no influence on society.
Mark Twain

If caught **without a stitch** in the great outdoors, one is *au natural.* If indoors and can strike a pose, one is **nude.** In the case of being **stark-ballock-naked** and in a compromising situation, one is **nekkid.*** No defense — beat a hasty retreat without the bugle call.

The Part that Goes Over the Fence Last

It is never necessary to use that three-letter word regardless whether it has been in use since the 12th century. Nor the four-letter one short for **buttocks.** Just say buttocks. Or **bottom, behind,** or **rear end** for heaven's sake. If that is just too simple and one feels the need to express oneself more floridly, we suggest **posterior, derriere, ampersand, parts behind, prat** (hence, pratfall), **differential, fanny, fleshy part of the thigh, blind cheeks, bum,** or **tushy.** However we would like not, one hears, of course, of **ying-yang, wazoo,** and **poop-chute.** Or if you prefer the cloak of Latin, *gluteus maximus.*

---

*This southern colloquialism, often preceded by "buck," is differentiated from naked thusly: "Naked" means you do not have any clothes on. "Nekkid" means you don't have any clothes on and you're up to no good.

There once was a woman from Mass
Who had an enormously large ass
when asked does it wiggle
she replied with a giggle
No, but it occasionally does pass gas.

The Endomorph

"A goodly bulk," Shakespeare also called it. But even on those rare occasions when an absolute description is unavoidable, however ample the **avoirdupois,** we believe **buffalo-butt, barge-assed,** or **hopper-hipped** are unnecessarily mean. **Weight-advantaged** would be discreet. With **corpulent, obese,** or **endomorphic,** one gets the **broad-beamed** picture. **Callipygian** or **Rubenesque** are downright complimentary.

It is a long-held defense for having an amply fleshed mate that one is assured of optimum warmth in the winter and shade in the summer. Conversely, lore tells of a guy of disturbingly low morals and poor initiative who only dates fat girls because he figures, "They don't have much willpower."

We are seeking out the purveyors of these stories in order to exact retribution.

 NOTE: Any abuse is allowable if it is indemnified by the "bless her heart" clause. The only criteria for its application is that one can either claim Southern heritage or manage a credible Southern drawl when it is employed: "That girl is so fat, bless her heart, if she sat on a bug it would fossilize in five minutes."

Clarification: In the South, a boy or a girl is anyone under the age of 60.

Ill-Favored by Nature

Whether or not a person looks like they **fell from the ugly tree and hit every branch on the way down,** one certainly would not want to make this observation within their earshot. If it becomes necessary to describe an **unprepossessing** person to a third party and one does not want to be

Never try to teach a pig to sing, it wastes your time and annoys the pig.
Proverb

> The Lord prefers common-looking people.
> That is the reason why he made so many of them.
>
> *Abraham Lincoln*

out-right deceptive, said person might be described as **unlovely, disagreeable to the eye,** or **a bit homely.** Do avoid **butt-ugly** at all costs (impolitic remarks have a nasty history of payback).

THE PAPER BAG RULE

If only one paper bag over the head is necessary to keep from frightening children, one is uncomely. Two paper bags, admittedly hard-featured. Three paper bags, o.k., butt-ugly. If the person in question is a close friend or relative, said person is plain but has a good personality.

Postscript: If one would chew off an arm in the morning to escape undetected from a one-nighter who looked all right when they said, "Last Call," that person is **Coyote Ugly** (owing to a coyote's supposed willingness to chew off a limb to get out of a steel-jaw trap).

In our western regions, if one looks a bit worse for the wear, one has been **rode hard and put up wet.** If this colloquialism needs explaining, then it would be wise not to try to work **that dog won't hunt** into the conversation either.

Short Pockets

A small-statured person is not **sawed-off** nor **suffering from duck's disease** (short legs), but is **vertically-challenged, abbreviated, a bit close to the ground, compact, diminutive, petite, slight, undersized, wee,** or **not tall.** Alternately one with exceedingly long legs may have **high pockets** and **run like a dromedary with the staggers,** but it would be kinder to describe him as **lean, lanky,** or **rangy.** She is **statuesque,** unless, of course she is a carbon copy of *Olive Oyl.* If this is the case, one might want to disregard **bony, emaciated, scrawny, living stick,** or **skeletal** and rely on **slender** or **a bit spare.**

Buck-Toothed

As to why the French describe someone with protruding teeth as *dents a l'anglaise,* we shall, in the name of diplomacy, not look to the British throne.

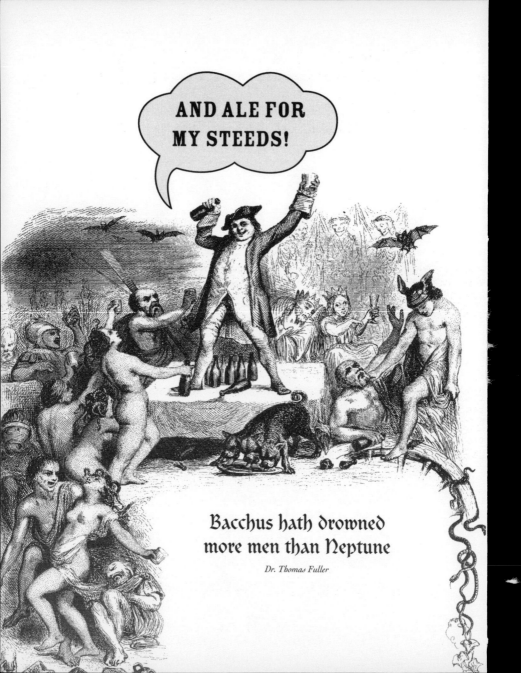

Worshipping at the Shrine of Bacchus

Killing a Few Brain Cells

Webster's first definition for **bibulous** is "highly absorbent," which is probably why its second definition describes one who over-imbibes on alcoholic substances. Over-imbibers are also: **besotted, befuddled, bleary-eyed, blotto, soused, bombed, Bosco Absoluto, adrip, afloat, wall-eyed, cup-shot, lit, likkered up, walking on rock socks,** or **stinking drunk.**

An **oenophile** is a lover of wine. With the addition of a prepositional phrase such as "of legendary proportions," said drinker is a **wino.**

The difference between a drunk and an alcoholic is that drunks don't have to attend all those meetings.

How we identify inebriates today is not half so eloquent as did our forefathers. Their excessive quaffers were called

The trouble with jogging
is that the ice falls
out of your glass.

belch-guts, bibblers, biled owls, bloaters, boosey-cocks, bubbing-culls, cadgers, fuddle-caps, fuddlers, grog-hounds, gullions, guttles, large-heads (a hands-down favorite), **lick-spigots, lick-wimbles, moist-uns, plonk-dots, squiffs,** and **tosspots.**

The productive drunk is the bane of moralists.

Anon

An alcoholic is someone you don't like who drinks as much as you.

Dylan Thomas

Paying for It

crapulous \'kra-pye-les\ adj [LL crapu-
losus, fr. L crapula intoxication, fr. Gk
kraipale] (1536) **1** : marked by intemperance esp. in eating or drinking
2 : sick from excessive indulgence in liquor

If not behind the wheel, **intemperance** can
be relatively benign. Indeed, a **crying jag**
is embarrassing but hardly lethal. Be fore-
warned, even **wearing beer goggles** (opti-
cally impaired by drink) can get a limb
chewed off (see **coyote ugly**). **In one's
armor (fighting drunk)** is the best way to
get **ass-whupped.** We don't even want to
talk about the infamous **brewer's droop** (also known as
whiskey dick). While **the morning after** one may be **spitting feathers,** visited by the **brown bottle flu** implies a trip
to **Europe with Ralph and Earl in a Buick.**

> *I always keep a stimulant handy in case
> I see a snake, which I also keep handy.*
> *W.C. Fields*

The **beezie-weezies** sound kind of cute. If you have
them it means an array of colorful visitors from the
animal kingdom have come to call on you **(pink
elephants, blue devils, red spiders, a black
dog,** or **snakes** — of any hue — **in one's boots).**

They are also synonymous with the **screaming meemies,** a term a tad more accurate. But the presence of either means the *delirium tremens* or **DTs** have invaded. And, if **on the wagon** is not something the afflicted has yet contemplated, clearly, the time is at hand.

✎FYI: *St. Bibiana,* 4th century Spanish
Patron Saint of hangovers

F its, disease, ill health, infirmity, breakdowns, affliction, ailment, attacks, bugs, collapse, complaint, confinement, convalescence, disability, disorder, disturbance, dose, failing health, flu, indisposition, malady, malaise, prostration, seizure, syndrome, a bit of unwell, and what's been going around

Indisposition

They do not fall under the canopy of saving face, litigation, nor feelings. No, these situations have to be the reason euphemisms were invented in the first place.

Gastro-Intestinal Disorder

Few of life's miseries have escaped schoolyard ridicule, occasionally even put to rhyme. Therefore, it is not surprising that **lower intestinal disturbance** inspired at least one school-age ditty — *"When you're sliding into home and your pants are full of foam, diarrhea, diarrhea . . ."*

There is an array of frank terms that describe not the bowel disorder itself, but the rapid response it necessitates. Hence, far too often we hear the **runs, quickstep, sprints, trots, scoots, scatters,** etc. Yet, admittedly, any of these are preferable to excusing oneself to company by declaring onset of the **screaming shits.** Additionally, if on one's vacation one has an attack of the **turistas,** assigning specific ethnic blame

Going to Europe with Ralph and Earl in a Buick

If one is sick to one's stomach, we believe that is all the information one needs to share. Throwing up or vomiting are also perfectly good descriptive terms. It has been our experience, once that announcement has been made, everyone pretty much gets out of your way on the way to the lavatory.

We reduce ourselves to the indelicacy of delineating regurgitation euphemisms for no other reason than it is an absolute playground for onomatopoetic words such as **gurk, urp,** and **barf.** With one's head stuck down the **big white phone,** one can **talk to Earl, Ralph,** or **Cousin Sis, call Hughie** or **cry Ruth.**

Invariably, the most colorful are offered up by friends of the vomitee recounting the entire event to avid listeners: **flash the hash, flay the fox, feed the fish, drive the Buick, bow to the porcelain altar, hug the throne, toss tacos, woof cookies, laugh at the carpet, launch one's lunch, de-food, bestow a Technicolor yawn, heave Jonah, blow beets, park a custard,** or **go see the Duchess of York.**

Evidently, there is bovine sub-category provision for the escalation of vomiting: to **bison** (be nauseated), **yak** (very nauseated), or **water buffalo** (throw up one's toenails).

such as **Montezuma's revenge, Dehli-belly, Mexican two-step, Spanish squirts, Botswana bop,** or **Cairo crud** does nothing to improve international goodwill.

Let's face it, unless one is sitting on the edge of an examining table wearing nothing but a gaping hospital gown, "I am unwell," is pretty much all anyone needs to tell.

Pussyfooting around The Curse

When **OTR (on the rag)** or having that **time of the month,** few occurrences engender more verbal pussyfooting (again, no pun intended) than **women's troubles.**

Victorian ladies suffered from **domestic affliction.** So general a term, however, could mean either the sink is stopped up or one's husband is a cur. Today we seldom hear of the **flowers, floods, vapors, wretched calendar,** or **high tide.**

While weathering **feminine complaint,** then as now, not only can one **entertain the general** or **fly the red flag,** one can have **the painters in, a wet weekend, endure wallflower week,** or a **visit from Aunt flo.** When the British **have landed** (wearing red coats), **the Captain is at home** and it is **BENO time** (there'll be no fun).

Inevitably, the onset of one's menstrual period requires **covering the waterfront** by the wearing of a **sanitary**

Fits, disease, ill health, infirmity, breakdowns, affliction,

product. It is preferable to specify **perineal pad** or **tampon** by brand name (Kotex, Tampax, etc.), else one is left with a hopeless number of riding analogies: the **cotton bicycle, red stallion, white sling, white horse,** or **fanny mattress.**

From a male point of view, this item is identified as **peter-cheater** or **manhole cover** which, while applicable, are in poor taste. **Pleasure garden padlock** sounds oh-so-refined, but we haven't conjured an occasion when this, as a topic of general conversation, was.

Crawling Creatures

When once only an accusation one screamed at the opposite sex at recess, **cooties** have become a renewed nuisance, not only to school children, but to the population in general. (There are those who blame this phenomenon entirely on the hippie generation.) One would think such progress would have birthed a parallel vocabulary. That seems not the case. Euphemisms for **pediculosis,** while dated, are interesting: **light troops, active citizens, bosom chums, familiars, walking dandruff, intimate friends,** and **seam squirrels.**

NOTE: **Lobby lice** are found in hotels, but of the two-legged variety, not eight.

Genital or crab lice are **crotch pheasants** and **pants rab-bits.** Lice are **chats,** hence, technically, a **chatty** person is not loquacious, but slovenly.

That nightly admonition to not let them bite not withstand-ing, few of us ever encounter bedbugs anymore. To the Victorians, they were a fact of life, yet a troubling conun-drum. The more fastidious citizens of society refused to ut-ter the word "bug" because of its unfortunate connotation (see **The Love That Durst Not Speak Its Name**). Hence, the pesky critters were known as **gentlemen in brown, B-flats,** or **Norfolk Howard** (which may or may not refer-ence either the War of the Roses or Flodden Field — far too obscure for a non-Anglophile to ascertain).

Social Diseases

Disgraceful disorders refer specifically to gonorrhea (the **clap**) and syphilis (the **pox**). Other substitutes are: **bad blood, nasty complaint, bone ache, foul disease, deli-cate taint, pintle fever, fire down below, forget-me-not, Venus' curse,** and **infinite malady.** Historically, however, such misfortune appears to have incited unlimited oppor-tunity to disparage various ethnicities: **French measles, Neapolitan favor, Spanish gout, Irish mutton,** and **Rangoon itch.**

Foul Emanations

There once were two men in black suits
who had trouble controlling their poots
At lunch one finally said
As the other nodded his head
We should switch now from beans to fruits

Breaking Wind

Should one **befoul the air** with an unduly emphatic noise, one has committed a **rouser.** If one got by, it was a **blind-fart** also known the acronym **SBD**— silent but deadly. Anything in between is a **backfire, backdoor trumpet, bad powder, buck-snort,** or **bathtub bubble.** In addition, a **whistle britches** can suffer **butter's revenge** or **pocket thunder.**

This is the rankest compound of villainous smell that ever offended nostril.

Shakespeare

Under these audible circumstances (if the dog is unavailable to blame), someone might have **stepped on a frog, talked German** (supposed guttural reference), **cut a rusty, sliced the cheese,** or **shot rabbits.** If any of these aforementioned indiscretions occur and the offender does not know to look suspiciously at others, then that person does not deserve to inhabit polite society.

As already observed, when one is beset by gastrointestinal disorder, there is little discretionary reaction time. We shall assume any **sullying of the air,** too, is inadvertent, giving all transgressors (you know who you are) blanket clemency.

There once was a wonderful wizard
who had a great pain in his gizzard
So he ate wind and snow
at 50 below
and farted a forty day blizzard.

FYI: Breaking wind was actually a great party trick in the Renaissance. Even Dante wrote of a *fartiste* who made a **trumpet of his ass.** At the turn of last century, a French nightclub performer, Joseph Pujol, reportedly plied his artistry in the Moulin Rouge. Although known to play *O Solo Mio* on the ocarina, his *tour de force* was an anal rendition of *Claire de Lune.*

Dog Breath

If one's breath is **strong enough to carry coal,** could **fell a horse at twenty paces,** or **smells like the Chinese army has walked through one's mouth in their sweat socks,** one has **halitosis.**

Some small woodland creature sneaked into his mouth and used it as a latrine.

In the Privy

Calls of Nature

In Elizabethan time, the place of ease was known as a **jakes**, this was eventually corrupted to **ajax.** Derivation of another more oft used term for *the facilities*, **the loo** remains under disagreement. Some like **l'eau** (French for water), others insist it lieu (as in "place"). Nonetheless, euphemisms for the room that contains a toilet can fall into two categories. In the first, based on the concept of contrary connotation, we have **bank, chapel, coffee shop, commons, counting house, cottage, library, office, parliament, Spice Island,** or the **temple.**

The less verbally discriminating, however, relieve themselves in a **bog, cacatorium, can, compost hole, dilberry creek, dunny, forakers, john, necessarian, place where one coughs, siege-house,** or **stool of ease.** In most places in Europe, one seeks the **W.C.** (water closet), which seems infinitely more reasonable than in America's **restroom** (where one may sit but does not necessarily rest).

FYI: Yes, the story is apparently true, there actually was a Thomas **Crapper** who invented a flush toilet.

Wring Out One's Socks

Our study has revealed a vast disparity
between the number of euphemisms for
male urination (lots) compared to those
for female (zilch). This may well fall to
the unquestionably finer sensibilities prevalent amongst the
lady-folk. Either that or if one sits to release one's bladder,
it is a solitary, quiet event. There is very little associated
activity once one has made certain the toilet seat is down.
But he who has a penis with which to pee can even write
his name in the snow — well, for argument's sake, we suppose a woman could do it, but it would take a while.

Men can also take the **snake for a gallop, siphon the
python, shake hands with the bishop, point Percy at the
porcelain,** or **train Terrance on the terracotta** after which
they can **shake the dew off the lily.**

Either sex could **give the Chinaman a music lesson,** but in
that few use china pots in which to tinkle anymore, it is
generally obsolete.

As an exit excuse to **relieve themselves,** men go **water the
horses, feed the goldfish, see how high the moon is, kill a
snake, chase a rabbit, drain the radiator,** or **check the ski
rack.** Women seem to just go to the "Ladies" to **powder
their noses** (albeit a bit nonsensically, in pairs).

☞ NOTE: There was a hunt-themed restaurant that initiated some baffled head-scratching among their patrons by labeling their respective restrooms, **Pointers** and **Setters.**

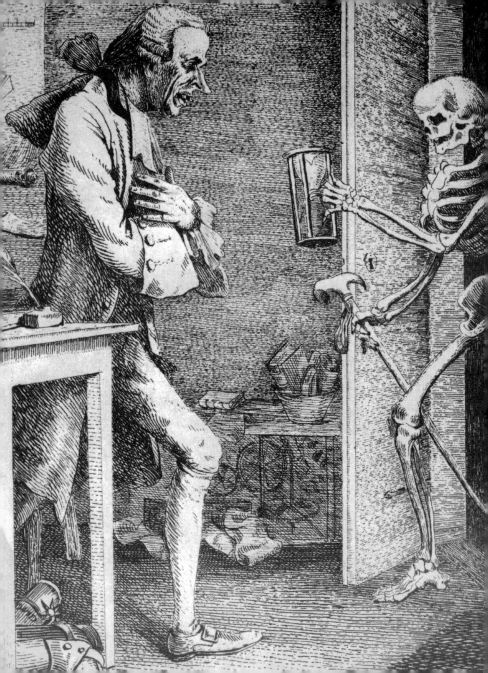

Afflicted by Time's Wing'd Chariot

Be kind to your children, they will choose your nursing home.

For those of us middle-aged (assuming everyone lives to be 110), **a person of maturity** has **the dwindles**, is **a bit forward at the knees, long in the tooth, white-topped, blue-haired, rusting out, old as the hills, in one's dotage,** and **no spring chicken,** whiling away their time in **God's waiting room.**

CAUTION: Make very certain the **senior citizen** of whom one speaks is **deaf as a post** before one utters any of these little nuggets. Else, the person upon whom one remarks is always **distinguished.**

He is alive, but only in the sense that he can't be legally buried.
Geoffrey Madan (subject of the observation unknown)

The Bucket Kick'd

Are there any grander occasions to pull out all the stops, euphemistically speaking, than speculating on just where the **dearly departed's** place of eternal rest will be? The **late-lamented** could land in **Abraham's bosom, be church triumphant, called to a higher service,** or, less optimistically, **stoking Lucifer's fires.** Non-ecumenically, a *quietus* or an *exitus* could have occurred.

Better judgment would insist (at least insofar as the eulogy) one avoid calling the deceased either **worm food** or **buzzard meat.**

Pardon My Dust

Dorothy Parker's epitaph by
Dorothy Parker

There appears to be a paradoxical inclination by the bereaved to insist said worm food to action when they have had **a mortality experience** (a term popular with the mortuary profession). Hence, we hear the dearly departed may **suck grass, grin at daisy roots, buy the farm, give up the ghost, pay nature's debt, pull a cluck, cash in one's chips, fold one's hand, coil one's rope, drop off the hook,**

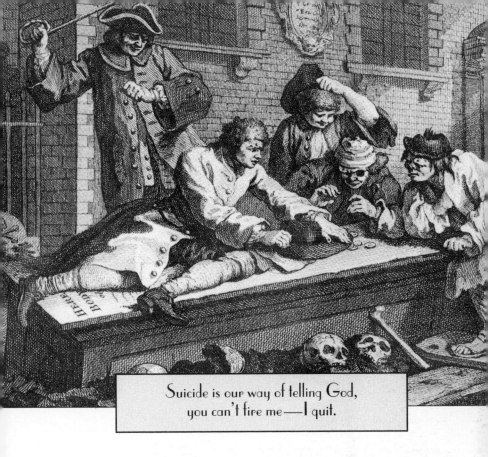

Suicide is our way of telling God,
you can't fire me — I quit.

slip the cable, sun one's moccasins, take the long count, jump the last hurdle, drop the cue, ride off on the last round-up, or answer the ever-lasting knock.

The report of my death was an exaggeration.

Mark Twain, after reading his own obituary, June 2, 1897

One of the funniest of Monty Python's routines involved the return of a dead parrot, "Maybe he's just **shagged out after a long squawk** — no, he's **bleeding demised, ceased to be, bereft of life, joined the choir invisible . . .**"

One can go **wearing the Q** (the death face rather coarsely delineated by comics — tongue lolling out the corner of the mouth), **feet first, toes up, eyes closed, heels foremost, face turned to the wall, on one's shield, in a box,** or **in repose** . . . whence one goes to the **bone orchard.**

Gender specific activity, femininity, manhood, manliness, masculinity, sexuality, womanhood, womanliness, intercourse between animate beings, coition, coitus, copulation, *fornication, generation, magnetism, procreation, relations, reproduction, sensuality, sexuality* intimacy, lovemaking,

Bed is the poor
man's opera.
Italian Proverb

Bewitched, Bothered and Betwattled

Overborne by Desire

Few, if any, still believe that only the male gender suffers from the **pangs of lust.** If proof be needed, the phenomena of Valentino, Elvis and Chippendale's dancers provide full support for the theory that **sexual appetence** is an equal opportunity employer. Yet, regardless how prevalent its use, we again point out that the word **horny,** via horn, comes from a root word pertaining to the erect penis. Therefore, for absolute accuracy, a woman may be just as **lustful, dissolute, concupiscent, lascivious, libidinous, salacious, appetent, licentious, ribald, prurient, wanton,** or **humpy** as a man, but, unless born a hermaphrodite, or completed gender reassignment, she will not be horny.

Those terms describing the **throes of excess cupidity** can be gender specific and — however we wish they not — the examples that come to mind for men are **pussy simple, cunt-struck** and **betwattled.** Although a woman may **have**

hot pants or be **cocksmitten,** we prefer to say either is **confounded by love** (more likely confounded by lust, but it is not our place to proselytize). The unmistakable (and most conspicuous) concomitant of desire, however, is borne by the male: *Penis in erectus.*

Temporary Priapism

Although it might initially sound like a Viagra high, a **priapism** (named after Priapus, a Greek and Roman god of male generative power) is a medical condition that manifests itself by an unrelenting erection which is quite painful and—here's the catch—is unrelieved by sexual gratification. We will remark only upon the temporary kind.

Unlikely as it is to be referenced in one of Martha Stewart's fine books, for procreative (or recreational) purposes everyone will agree that an erection is **A Good Thing.** However, if the little devil rears its head when copulation is merely on the mind but not imminent, it might prompt some explaining—something we did not find indexed by Miss Manners either.

If a **rise in one's Levi's** is espied by someone peripheral to the action, we advise the male in question to adopt an air of innocence and complain of an **involuntary biological reaction. Genital tumescence, virile reflex,** and **male arousal** are equally non-accusatory terms. All are preferable to **hat rack, blue-veiner, clothes prop, tent peg, live rabbit, proud meat, horn colic, bit of a stiff,** or **sporting some wood**—even if one is **ready to dig post holes with it.**

☞ NOTE: Many men consider an inadvertent **hard-on** (an expression we do not endorse) as an unwitting condition and maintain, therefore, that they should not be held accountable for that over which they hold no control (see **The Unruly Member**).

Certainly beyond one's sway is **morning pride,** which, for exonerative purposes, can be identified as **matutinal erection.** Indeed, if the male can convey an appropriately sleepy-headed look, this excuse is good until noon. If one's **nocturnal erection** is inexplicably relieved during the night, one has **shot the bishop.**

Another actual affliction is **erethism,** an abnormal irritability or responsiveness to stimulation. Erethism (it too comes from Greek, but we did not find any reference to the god of crankiness) is an actual disorder, which does give marginal credibility to the otherwise questionable assertion by some men that for arousal they need no more inducement than a stiff breeze. One could propose either of these ailments as reason for undue . . . excitement, but both are a bit obscure. We suggest one assert oneself as **constitutionally inclined to passion.** It sounds a bit Edwardian, but far better than **randy as a goat.**

BEWARE: If one needs to call upon this explanation while wearing nothing more than a trench coat, it is probable the police will look upon one's suffering unsympathetically. The docket sheet will read lewd conduct, however, not **weenie-wagger.**

Is that a gun in your pocket — or are you just glad to see me?
Mae West

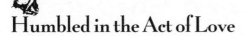

Humbled in the Act of Love

Alternately, if the male **member** remains **flaccid** regardless of encouragement, he is suffering from **orgiastic impotence.** He has not only **failed in the furrow,** he has **no money in his purse, lead in his pencil, ink in his pen,** nor **toothpaste in his tube.** When his ability is thus compromised, he is **slack in his matrimonial duty** or **leaving the pillow unprest.** The culprit is itself **deadwood, a dangling participle, dolphin, flounder, lob-cock, half-mast, flat tire, hanging Johnny,** or **Mr. Softy.**

The Long Carbine

Whether one is endowed with a howitzer or peashooter, guns are, and always have been, phallic symbols.

In the 17th century, flintlock guns had a hammer, a flint to produce a spark, a lockpan that held the priming powder

and a main charge behind the musket ball. When the hammer was released, it hit a small flint rock igniting a spark that lit the priming powder, and if all went as planned, then exploded the main charge. Sometimes this pre-high-tech procedure backfired and the priming powder flashed but did not ignite the main charge. Hence a flash in the pan, but no shot was produced. If one had game (or the enemy) in one's sights but needed time to aim, the hammer could be partially cocked. If the gun fired while in this position, it went off half-cocked — no doubt a quite vexing and dangerous occurrence.

We recount all of this seeming arcane information only to provide background to fully understand the following:

If one achieves an erection but one's intention is thwarted by a premature ejaculation, one has **gone off half-cocked, fired in the air, shot in the bush, misfired,** or has experienced **a flash in the pan. Hanging fire** occurs when the priming powder initially failed to ignite the main charge. This term has come to be synonymous with indecision, not as some insist, a lengthy orgasm. These expressions have been bandied about for both sexual and non-sexual purposes for centuries. When we study their origins, they do make perfect sense.

Sometimes a cigar is just a cigar.
Attributed to Sigmund Freud

As much as it sounds as if it should be, we all know to **peter-out** is not necessarily a sexual innuendo. In fact, the dictionary definitions for peter are as follows: (1) to diminish, (2) to become exhausted, (3) a vulgar name for one's penis, and (4) one of the twelve apostles. (Insomuch as one's penis (3) diminishes (1) when it becomes exhausted (2), we will conclude that other than that the Apostle Peter (4) must have had one, he is irrelevant to this discussion).

The French word *pete* means to explode weakly (also an expulsion of intestinal gas). ***Peter dans la main*** means literally, to come to nothing. *The Dictionary of Word Origins* says that peter-out originated with miners in the mid-1800's (an explanation of which, trust us, is even less relevant than the Apostle Peter). Regardless, what we do know is that to **peter-out** means to give out—be spent—and usually not with a bang (so to speak). Lest one's lover be **unconsoled,** we suggest it is time to explore **The French Arts.**

If one can **get it up,** but is sterile—**firing blanks,** or engaging in a **dry bob,** one is **improcreant.**

AGRICULTURAL SIDEBAR

For those unaware, when a horse and a donkey mate, their offspring is a mule, a hybrid. This hybrid cannot reproduce; hence, one occasionally hears an improcreant male referred to as a **mule.**

Dallying,
Firkytoodling, and
Finkdiddling

If one has **the Jones for** another, as a rule, one dares not **jump their bones** without first introducing oneself. Under the right circumstances, small talk can be dispensed with, but it is reasonable to insist that if copulation is the goal, at least a little foreplay is in order. This is known as **canoodling.**

Engaging in **tonsil hockey, chewing face,** and **cow kissing** means, in baseball analogy, one has arrived at **first base. Copping a feel** above the waist is a **double.** The digital investigation of a female's privates (otherwise known as **down there**) is a **bit for the finger** and progression to **third base** (a hand down a man's pants is probably third base also, but one seldom hears women using sports analogies). Reasonably, **physical congress** is **going all the way,** because one has **scored** (yes, scored) a **home run.**

If one ruts on another without penetration or relocation of one's clothing, it is called a **dry hump** and runners do not advance to home. Male students of an Ivy League school perform the **Princeton rub** and, we are told, **no one scores** (bats, if not balls, being optional).

Making the Beast with Two Backs

To have a legion of suitable euphemisms for **doing the big nasty** at one's fingertips, there is a very simple formula.

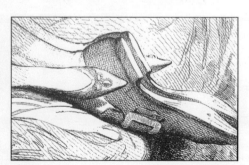

Merely select any combination of an adjective from the first column and noun from the second. *Voila!*

Adjective	Noun
Physical	congress
Carnal	knowledge
Intimate	necessities
Capital	embrace
Amorous	favors
Connubial	attention
Passionate	connection
Fulfilling	arrangements
Horizontal	relief
Illicit	affections
Nocturnal	pleasures
Conjugal	union
Voluptuous	combat
Loving	consummation
Secret	deed
Lewd	rites
Naughty	conflict
Night	association
Nuptial	coupling

When in want of euphemistic eloquence, however, we often rely on Latin as in *in coitu* or *actus coitus*. Shakespeare's words, however, are positively rhapsodic: **The very lists of love, to make one's heaven in a lady's lap, dance on one's heels, lay it to one's heart,** or **behind door work.** Indeed, **having an enseamed** or **fortunate bed** sounds a skosh classier than **parking the pink mustang up a side street.** Granted, Shakespeare was capable of circumlocutory stretch. **Groping for trout in a peculiar river** means fishing in a private stream, which means **knowing someone in the Biblical sense.** Knowing someone in the Biblical sense means that one is engaging in an **act of generation, androgyny** (no, not Boy George — at least not necessarily), **original sin, shame, darkness,** or, in the words of Delbert McClinton, **plain ol' makin' love.**

We Are Not Amused

In Victorian times, **illicit love** referred to sexual shenanigans between anyone outside of holy wedlock. So heinous was such activity, it was called **criminal conversation** (a more stupefyingly cryptic euphemism we have yet to behold). If it became necessary to allude to such **foul doings** in print, even so ambiguous a term as criminal conversation was far too explicit. It was abbreviated as **crim. con.** or even **c.c.,** a ruse that was not particularly effective.

Sociologists explain that sexual shenanigans inside holy wedlock were frowned on as well, but we understand that authorities were seldom able to actually make arrests for it.

Wreak One's Passion

If our ancestors' sensibilities in print were euphemized into total obscurity, private conversations were not held to the same standard. We note that the designation for the act of **c.c.** was then, as now, often pre-ceded by an acquiring verb: **getting, having, copping, grabbing, nab-bing, snatching, fetching, wanting,** and occasionally, **begging** for any noun used to specify the female *pu-dendum.* Typical of these nouns are **cookie, nooky, ass, beaver, bird, jam, pork, bob, snug, box, bull's eye, buns, booty, cat, pussy, crack, cranny, crotch, down, flesh, hole, fur-pie, honey-pot, kitty, lap, milk, monkey, mouse, muff, naughty, oyster, poontang, rump, squirrel, twat, twittle,** and **you-know-what** (often times further identified ad-jectively as **a bit of**). All are, even now, substituted for the detested "c" word.*

* Although it has been in use since the 14th century, we offer less sensibility stun-ning euphemisms for the **monosyllable** under the heading **The Little Man and His Boat.**

87

On occasion, this vast array of monosyllabic choices causes an exceedingly aroused male to abandon assigning what he wants a specific name. He may eliminate the use of a noun altogether and just says **some** (get some, want some, etc). However brainless this sounds, we have to give credit here. Although man is an unwitting party, Webster's does define the word *some* as "being an unknown, undetermined, or un-specified unit or thing." This suggests that when **in rut**, the male of the species does not like to restrict his possibilities.

To Spend

If referring to the male **orgasm, shot his wad, blown off, spooged,** or **popped his nuts** are unnecessary. He has ex-perienced **sexual reflex.** He can also have **eventuation,**

emissio seminis, or **effect emission** (although we admit the latter does sound a bit like a NASA instruction). For women, **making the chimney smoke** seems not overly graphic, but again, we prefer the French, *petit mort* meaning **little death. Come, spend,** and **get off** do refer to orgasm for both sexes, but then, so does **climax.**

The Loving Spoonful

That which is ejaculated, is just that, **ejaculate. Baby batter, duck butter, man oil, bull gravy, gism, guma glue, buttermilk,** and **love juice** are a bit too . . . *icky.* We prefer it called **semen, reproductive fluid,** or even **sexual discharge.**

Leukorrhea is the whitish viscid discharge from the vagina known more delicately as *fleurs blanches* or **white flowers.** (In the 19th century, wags said this condition was occasioned by young ladies who read overly explicit French novels.) Those less discerning call it the **twitters.** Only the outright crude would pronounce her **dripping for it.** Under the heading of untoward euphemisms, we find **snail trails** (the resultant traces of vaginal secretion on a woman's leg) and **pecker tracks** (dribbles of semen on trousers — or, occasionally, a blue dress).

Prithee, summon ye laundress.

The cheesy sebaceous matter that collects around the *glans penis* and the foreskin or the clitoris and *labia minora* is neither **gnat bread** nor **crotch cheese**. It is **smegma** (granted, a word that sounds only marginally better than crotch cheese). In the fairer sex, this is understood to be **too much cheese on the taco** and an indication of better attention to personal hygiene.

> Between two evils,
> I always pick the one
> I never tried before.
> *Mae West*

Bow at the Altar of Eros

One should try every experience once,
excepting incest and folk-dancing.

Arnold Bax

In some societies, anything other than the missionary position (*figura veneris primi*) between a **churched couple** is
not only considered kinky but illegal. The ancient legend
of **The Dragon and St. George** notwithstanding, doing it
dorsally (*coitus a la vache*) or **doggy-style** will get you jail
time. But, if the woman is on her back (**star-gazing**) and
the man on top (**beating the bunny**), evidently the kitchen
table is just fine so long as the kids are asleep.

Chinese fashion denotes a sexual arrangement found in
ancient woodcuts revealing the male and the female facing
each other in an entwined X configuration. This reference
is tainted by its association with some rather tasteless jokes
proposing it necessary to copulate with an Asian woman in
such a fashion because her **pudendal crevice** is supposedly
horizontal.

Q. Why don't Frenchmen like to eat flies?

A. Because they can't get their little legs apart.

Different Strokes

There once was a girl from Vancouver
Whose mouth had the strength of a Hoover;
When she turned it on high,
A week would pass by,
Before anyone could remove her.

Q. What is the definition of trust?

A. Two cannibals giving each other a blow job.

In popular vernacular, a **blow job, talking to mike, polishing the helmet, giving head,** or **lipstick on the dipstick** denotes **achieving sexual satisfaction through oral stimulation.** Either sex can be a **goot-gobbler, piccolo player, peter-eater, lick spigot, dicky-licker,** or **mouth-whore** (one particularly well-practiced is said to be able to **suck the chrome off a trailer hitch**). Introduce the use of Latin and a modicum of class drapes any **non-orthogenital sex** act no matter how indelicate: *penilingus, fellatio,* or *irrumatio* (root word, to suck). We add that a female who **fellates** is a **fellatrice.**

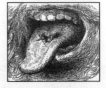

Talking to the canoe driver, nose painting, sneezing in the basket, yodeling in the canyon, gamahuching, whistling in the dark, eating at the Y, having a hairburger, mouth music, lickety-split, and **muff-diving** mean *cunnilingus.* (As this activity is not new, it is not surprising that those mutton-chop sideburns were called **depth markers** long before the sixties.) **Loop de loop, 69,** or *soixante neuf* is **mutual oral-genital stimulation.** Two women involved in such activity are engaged in **bird-washing.**

Granted, **shooting the beaver** (or, **squirrel**, or **moon**) could pertain to a night out with one's favorite scent hound, but most likely it references **female exhibitionism.** Alternately, a female-attired male prostitute **hides his candy** (and occasionally said candy is discovered by an un-amused client). **Goober-grabber** usually means a forward woman. We note however, that goobers can be grabbed by either sex. Sadly, we can offer no socially acceptable euphemisms for these last entries.

93

The Love That Durst Not Speak Its Name
or the Unmentionable Vice

Paedictcato, crimen innomentatum, coitus in ano — gay sex is still called **buggery** in some circles. Also, *concubitus cum persona ejus dem sexus*, **alternative proclivities**, or **same-sex-oriented**. (Although the receiver in this act has been called a **pillow-biter**, we find that distinction to be pan-sexual.)

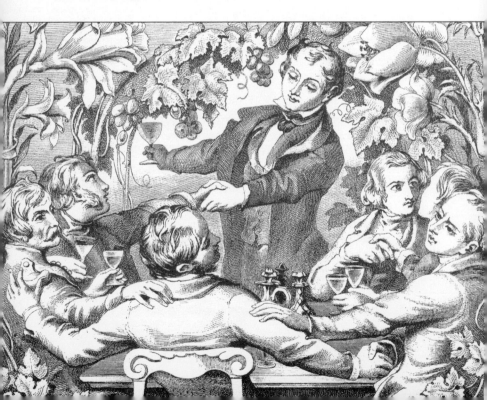

In the unlikelihood one finds it necessary to note the sexual inclinations of another, we hold that it is best to cleanse one's euphemistic repertoire of the terms **Nancy-boy, friend of Dorothy's** (referencing Parker, not *the Wizard of Oz* — although one's confusion on this point might be understandable), **confirmed bachelor, light in the loafers, playing for the pink team, pouff,** and **no bull-fighter. Sissybritches** and **pantywaist,** along with **manhole inspector,** or **rump ranger** should also be avoided. **Gunsel** (derivation of the German for gosling) is passably PC if the person to whom one refers is also a jerk.

Daisy (along with **daffodil** and **pansy**) has long been used as an insulting term for a gay man. That notwithstanding, participation in a **daisy chain** would involve a group of like-minded individuals engaging in simultaneous, er, sexual acts.

☞**FYI:** It was not until the second decade of the twentieth century that the word **faggot** came to be a disparaging term for a male homosexual. In the middle ages, faggot meant a bundle of sticks, and, understandably, **fag** eventually became slang for cigarette. In the 1800's, it also meant to work hard or become exhausted (by having to cut all that fire wood?). Its contemporary connotation possibly stems from its use to describe the tradition of young English boarding school boys who act as a servant to older students. The rumors about what actually occurs in single-sex schools when hormones rage undoubtedly fanned the fires of this particular vulgarism.

As for her, she may be somewhat **butch,** but **rug-muncher, lesbyterian,** and **bull-dyke** are understandably offensive. (For further aspersions on masculine women, see *Dog City.*)

Switch Hitting

If one has taken a position of non-discrimination about the sexual orientation of one's romantic encounters, one is referred to on the street as **ambisextrous, double-gaited, batting and bowling, AC-DC, trolling both sides of the stream, driving a two-way street,** or **buttering both sides**

of the bread. We, however, insist said person is influenced by an *amphi-genous* inversion.

Fetishes and General Freakiness

A widow whose singular vice
was to keep her late husband on ice.
Said "It's been hard since I lost him—
But, I'll never defrost him!
Cold comfort, but cheap at the price."

A hundred years ago the learned did not call pornography **smut,** but **facetiae** or **curiosa.** By the twentieth century, an abnormal interest in obscene material was known as **coprophilia,** although more technically that is the use of feces for sexual excitement. Those who revel in such activity are indelicately referred to as **fecal-freaks, kitchen cleaners,** and **felch queens.** To **felch** means to perform **anilingus*** (**tookus-lingus** to our less somber fellow beings). A **pound cake-queen** enjoys being defecated on. Anyone engaged in this base pastime (beyond the age of two) is taking part in a **Boston Tea Party.** An associated activity, **golden showers,** is more formally termed **micturation.** (Our informa-

---

*If one needs it spelled out, anilingus is to the anus what cunnilingus is to the cun . . . er, vagina.

tion notwithstanding, polite society prefers that if these . . . entertainments exist, they pass unremarked.)

Apparently, there is a "queen" designation to fit every manner of sexual diversion. For instance, one who is under the spell of a **foot fetish** (*equus eroticism*) is known as a **shrimp-queen** (referring to the shape of the toes), enjoys sex in the great outdoors: a **green-queen,** or in public: a **tea room-queen.**

Once: a philosopher, twice: a pervert!"

Voltaire
(turning down his second invitation to an orgy)

If generously lubricated by cooking oil, your run-of-the-mill orgy is a **Mazola party. Team cream, gang bang, round pound,** and **bunch punch** appear self-explanatory — this poetry occurring, undoubtedly, when one **trots out one's pussy** to **pull a train,** or **choo-choo.**

Said the masochist to the sadist: "Beat me, beat me!"

Replied the sadist: "No."

Originally, ascetics employed ritual floggings to induce discipline through strict self-denial by means of **mortification of the flesh.** Evidently, somewhere in this mix of flogging and religious frenzy, sexual titillation reared its ubiquitous head. Pious monks in robes metamorphosed into leather-clad dominatrices wielding wicked-looking whips. Indeed, if one has not actually experienced it, one has certainly heard of being **whipped into a frenzy.**

My problem is reconciling my gross habits to my net income.

Attributed to Errol Flynn

There is **bondage** and **sado-masochism.** In bondage one finds erotic stimulation either in exacting or under subjugation. One who finds sexual satisfaction by inflicting pain on another is a **sadist** — not **slap artist** nor **fire-queen** (not to be confused with a **flaming-queen** who is a relatively benign, if outrageously flamboyant, male homosexual).

Flagellation (not to be confused with flatulence — although it is noted that foundered horses used to be flogged in order to force them to pass gas) can be inflicted either by a willing compatriot or one's own hand. Indeed, a **masochist** gets off by being beaten literally or figuratively. And while most people know that sadism found its name by way of the infamous Marquis DeSade, few realize masochism

was named for the German novelist, Leopold von Sacher-Masoch who evidently also wrote of what he lived.

NOTE: There is the term **Zooerasty,** but we decided that there is some information we just do not want to have. Clearly, however, limerick writers have been much amused with the notion.

The Right Reverend Dean of St. Just
Was consumed with erotical lust
He buggered three men
Two mice and a hen
And a little green lizard that bust.

101

Sex "Sain et Sauf"

One may hear of **peek-freaks** and **peer-queers,** but they are *voyeurs.* If one gets one's jollies by listening, one is an *ecouteur.*

Dishearten

If a man is sexually aroused and then brought to satisfaction by manual manipulation of his member by another, he has been **brought down by hand,** a more circumspect term for a **hand-job, spitting white,** or **upshot.** (The person who supplied the hand is a **peter-beater** who **caught an oyster** otherwise known as "sweetheart.")

No Glove — No Love

It has been some time since one would hear of a condom wearer as **fighting in armor.** So ancient is the term, it very nearly predates the invention of **circular protection** itself. It may surprise some to know that **condoms** were in use as early as Elizabethan times although they did not become common (and then only in the large cities) until two centuries later.

These early sheaths were often made of material such as sheepskin (ouch), fish bladder (yuck) and eventually, rubber. Indeed, Casanova is said to have bragged of owning a pretty little linen ditty (*un petit linges*) with a delicate drawstring ribbon — the upper class does have its privileges. Some of these early protectors were said to bear the portraits of famous persons — the significance of which does

animate beings, coition, coitus, copulation, fornication, generativ

103

not immediately leap to mind. Perhaps a modern equivalent is a lunch box bearing the image of Mighty Morphin' Power Rangers — but we suppose we digress.

Once these handy little devices were perfected, euphemisms did abound — **keeping down the census, taking a dry run,** or **wearing a cheater.** Wearing a **fearnought, lace curtain, diving suit, head gasket, nightcap, catcher's mitt, rubber cookie, overcoat, raincoat, saddle, shower cap, life-preserver, washer, party hat, Dutch cap, phallic thimble,** or, less preferably, a **cum drum** could reference either a condom, or a diaphragm. A **pussy butterfly** is an **intrauterine device** or **IUD.**

Most commonly, however, a **protective sheath** has been called, variously, a **French, Italian, Spanish,** or **American letter.** (We did not find indication that it has been called an **English letter.** Hmmm.)

Malthus was an English curate. The Maltusian Theory posits that population tends to increase geometrically and resources or means of subsistence, arithmetically. Hard-liners believed that unless procreation was checked by moral restraint or even disaster (pestilence, famine, or war) unrelenting poverty and its resultant human degradation would inevitably result. This doctrine is often cited as an excuse for the use of birth control, hence, labeling any non-procreant sex, **Malthusian.**

A vasectomy means not ever having to say you're sorry.

Sex a Cappella

The **rhythm method** may indeed be chancy, but it is still a bit graceless to refer to it as **playing Vatican roulette. Riding bareback** means intercourse **without protection.** On occasion, condom-less sex is called **making faces** in that it often leads to producing babies.

FYI: As the male anatomy is limited in its ability to produce semen rapidly, when a man is fortunate enough as to enjoy what is called a triple header, a fourth round might result in his **coming air.**

NOTE: In England if someone tells you to **keep your pecker up,** it is indeed an expression of encouragement. However, not necessarily what one imagines. In Great Britain, pecker can mean chin.

NOTE, PART 2: There was a big hoo-haw over there when the American movie *Free Willy* premiered because **willy** does not mean chin in England.

NOTE, PART 3: If fortune has smiled upon one to the extent that one has somehow missed seeing any of the Austin Powers' movies, please understand, in Great Britain, a **shag** is not a 70's haircut.

My wife doesn't understand me. We're only staying
together for the kids. I've never done this before. I only
shoot blanks. If you get pregnant, honey, I'll take care of you.
I'll respect you in the morning. I promise it won't come in your mouth.

Men Behaving Badly

Although **snatch** can be either verb or noun, in either sense it usually refers to rapid copulation. **Irish foreplay,** sometimes known as **brace yourself Bridget,** is essentially a **Wham Bam, Thank You Ma'am** with a lilt. **Jewish foreplay,** we have been told, involves only extended pleading. A **flyer** can be either prone or vertical. If an **upright quicky,** it is also known as a **knee-trembler.** Occasionally this excursion doesn't even entail intercourse. To **cop a feel** is either with or without permission and is usually performed **nose open** (for those unfamiliar with animal husbandry — it describes an eager bull) possibly **with it in his hand** (which clearly does not).

The check's in the mail. I'll call you.

If it need be said, we endorse neither the above behavior nor the euphemisms, we only offer them for elucidative purposes.

A Pea in the Pod

One need not call a gestating woman **knocked up**[*]. She is *enceinte,* **fecund,** or **expecting.** While we do not find **preggers** offensive, **round-wombed, about to find pups, apron-up, one is up the spout, a lap full,** or **a bun in the oven** do not offer the proper respect as does **experiencing a blessed event.**

[*]Again, this is a phrase to use judiciously in England. For there if a woman has been knocked up it means she has merely experienced someone rapping on her door. Whether or not that leads to a shotgun wedding is beyond our polite speculation.

Misbegotten

The word **bastard** was once solely a comment on one's happenstance of birth. Some say the word came from the French, *fils de bast* or packsaddle child. **Born on the wrong side of the blanket** (the foul event producing said infant taking place other than within the marriage bed) or **born in the vestry** (left on the church steps) were other roundabout ways of disparaging one's heritage. Also, a **counterfeit, wood colt, stall whimper,** *nullius filius,* or **side-slip** (as in oops). Producing a child out of wedlock to Shakespeare was to **tender a fool.** More specifically in the chain of generations, a child born **out of wedlock** to a mother

who was **of illegitimate birth** herself, was said to be a **bell-bastard.**

Today, the word bastard, as used in this sense is so out of fashion as to be irrelevant. Indeed, most probably all these euphemisms have been overridden by **"DNA test"** and **"child support payments."**

Unknown to Man

In historical romance novels, a virgin (depending on the genre) was either **picked, plucked, ruined, trimmed, deflowered,** or **devirginated.** When a sweet young thing succumbed to seduction, she was **persuaded to venery.** Until then she was a **chaste treasure, virgin patent,** or **rosebud,** possibly remaining that way by **wearing iron knickers.** Digital investigation of the vagina comes under

the heading of **heavy petting.** For anyone in need of exact terminology — in legalese, **carnal knowledge** is the slightest penetration of the vulva. If one is messing with **jail-bait,** one is looking at jail time.

Even if she **spends more time on her knees than a priest,** she is still technically a virgin — *a* **demi-vierge** — never having **gone all the way.** Indeed, if the results of recently published, if somewhat unscientific, polls are to believed, by today's standards, a fellatio generating enough suction to **suck a golf ball through a garden hose** would not be considered a sex act. We believe this is now known as **The Clinton Exculpation.**

In scholarly tomes, one may come across the term, *claustrum virginale.* This reference is a bit of a stretch in that claustrum is one of the four basal ganglia in each cerebral hemisphere that consists of a thin lamina of gray matter separated from the lenticular nucleus by a layer of white matter (whew). However, we believe it is more likely that it is derived from claustral — cloister.

Trafficking with Oneself

95% of people masturbate.
The other 5% just lie about it.

If there are no obliging friends about and one does not care to avail oneself of **commercial outlets** (brothels), **genital stimulation via phallengetic motion** may be the only alternative for one's sexual . . . disposal. Still condemned by many, the **solitary vice** has managed not only to survive, but flourish, even under the threat of blindness, insanity, hairy palms and your mother's (and the Church's) wrath.

> There was a young fellow from Yale
> Whose face was exceedingly pale.
> He spent his vacation
> In self-masturbation
> Because of the high price of tail.

Many believe masturbation is synonymous with **Onanism.** In the Bible, however, Onan's sin, scholars insist, was not masturbation at all but *coitus interruptus.* (Regardless, he was slain by God for this heinous sin and let that be a lesson to us all.) This misunderstanding may well have been a deliberate Victorian manipulation of the scriptures laying the groundwork for generations of adolescent guilt-trips.

Additionally, as Onan was a guy, these guilt-trips were taken primarily by young men. The Victorian rationale was that all womankind (wives, daughters, mothers—i.e. any female a Victorian man was not trying to seduce) were

chaste of mind and body. Indeed, most doctors of the era persisted with the fallacy that ladies were devoid of sexual desire; therefore, the possibility of these women having an orgasm with or without the aid of a penis did not exist. Hence, it is the masculine population whose indiscriminate nocturnal . . . twiddling came under intense scrutiny and abject condemnation. So strong was the shame, we still hear **self-pleasuring** condemned as **genital pollution, self-abuse,** and **the sin of youth.**

Wanking may be the more oft-used term, but for those formal occasions, **digitally oscillating one's penis** or **self-induced penile regurgitation** would be preferable. In French, *se branler, se crosser, se faire les cinq doigts de la main, se passer un poignet,* or *la veuve poignet* (branler — to shake, crosser — to club, faire — perform, cinq doigts — five fingers, passer — happen, poignet — wrist, veuve — widow — you do the math.) If merely **fiddling with the equipment,** one is **playing pocket pool.**

As the dogma surrounding this abhorrent act is so intense and the deed is fraught with such euphemistic eloquence, it is an absolute necessity to be generous in recounting them.

Take Herman to the Circus

The chasm separating proper Victorian sensibility and that of the unwashed masses about who was and was not the

Master of One's Domain (a term "Seinfeld" did not invent) can be succinctly defined. For every shaming euphemism, we find dozens that are unrepentant (and if not actually poetry, one can appreciate the rhyme): **bleed the weed, bang your wang, shake the snake, ram the ham, rope the Pope, spank the frank, squeeze the cheese, stroke the bloke, crank one's whank, flog the log, lube the tube, wanker the anchor, hone the cone, strain the vein, pump the stump, torque the fork, thump the pump, tickle the pickle, jerkin' the gherkin, yank your plank, tease the weasel, fist your mister, punchin' the munchkin** and **make the scene with a magazine.**

Some are, if not poetic, at least alliterative: **burp the baby, cuddle the Kielbasa, fondle the fig, punish Percy in the palm, smash the stake, hug the hog, stir one's stew, strangle the stogie, slap pappy, bash, beat, or bop the bishop, pummel the priest, wave the wand, whip one's**

wire, **paddle the pickle, bang the banjo, dash one's doodle, grip the gorilla,** and **prime one's pump.**

There are dated euphemisms—**get the German soldiers marching, have a date with Rosy Palms, polish one's helmet, phone the czar, take Herman to the circus, feed the ducks, clean one's rifle, give a one gun salute,** and **choke the sheriff and wait for the posse to come;** and contemporary—**adjust your set, go on Pee Wee's little adventure, boot up the hard drive, paint a small Jackson Pollock, stretch the turtleneck, play the single-string air guitar, feed the Kleenex, tweak your twinkie, do the Han Solo, romance the bone, choke Kojak, play Uno, R2 your D2, upgrade your hardware, test fire the love-rocket.**

There once was a man named McGill,
Whose acts grew exceedingly ill,
He insisted on habits,
involving white rabbits,
and a bird with a flexible bill.

The animal kingdom is not only not exempt, it is well represented: **gag the maggot, lope the mule, wax the dolphin, burp the worm, look for ticks,** and **corral the tadpoles.** Granted the prominent feature of euphemisms for this activity is hardly political correctness, a few examples would outright enrage PETA: **club the baby seal, violate the hedge-hog, flog the dolphin, suffocate the trout, pound the pup, pump the python,** or **choke the chicken.**

I swear, you could ask your class if they'd had sex with goats and the next thing you'd hear is somebody asking, 'Define sex.'

Overheard from a College Professor

Everything else falls into the category of **one-night stands:** come to grips with oneself, climb Mount Baldy, audition the finger puppets, beat the bald-headed bandit, do the five-finger solo, iron the wrinkles, make the bald man puke, shake hands with the unemployed, rough up the suspect, summon the genie, butter the corn, kill the snake, seed the rug, paint the ceiling, dig for change, fire the flesh musket, frost the pastries, mangle the midget, unload the gun, varnish the flagpole, and **cane the vandal.**

While amusing, none of the above makes quite the statement as does **address Congress.**

Searching for Spock

> Nymphomaniacal Jill
> Tried a dynamite stick for a thrill
> They found her vagina
> Way over in China
> And bits of her tits in Brazil

Contrary to popular opinion, self-pleasuring (even, experts say, obsessive self-pleasuring) is not unique to the male of the species. We note that masculine verbal images involve all manner of phallic symbols such as guns and beasts. Those feminine (aside from allusions to small furry creatures) are quite dissimilar. (These are offered, we swear, only for their sociological enlightenment value.)

There are culinary references—**preheat the oven, baste the beaver, grease the skillet, butter the muffin, skim the cream, sort the oysters, stir the cauldron, roll the dough, and stuff the taco.** In the aforementioned animal category—**caress the kitty, dunk the beaver, feed the bearded clam, fan the fur, make the kitty purr, roll the mink, floss the cat,** and **check the foxhole.** Specific to the feminine sex too are **dig for one's keys, candle bashing, apply lip gloss, dust the end table, air the orchid, do one's nails (also soak in Palmolive), get a stain out of the carpet, part the petals, polish the pearl, do something for chapped lips, gusset typing, unclog the drain, ride side-saddle, paddle the pink canoe, wake the butterfly,** and **work in the garden.**

Fare un ðitolino (Italian: to do a little finger)

Specific to **self-digitation** is to **drown the man in the boat, circle the knoll, flip through the pages, grope the grotto, leglock the pillow, null the void, read Braille, stroke the furnace, surf the channel, play the silent trombone, do the two-finger slot rumba, play solitaire, check one's oil, tickle one's fancy, tiptoe through the two-lips, check the status of the I/O port, bury the knuckle,** and **search for Spock.** Oh yes, females can rhyme too: **scratch the patch, scuff the muff, itch the ditch,** and **rubbin' the nubbin.**

Not specific to women, but peculiar to them is the **poly-morphously perverse orgasm** where the entire body, not

122

just its genitals, is a source of erotic pleasure. Without direct clitoral stimulation, some women say **psychic orgasm** can be achieved. All one needs is either a risqué novel or a full bladder. No doubt, euphemisms have been coined just for such occurrences, but we are still digesting the information.

Pokin' the Pucker

The word **dildo** has been in use since the 16th century, but there is evidence the item was created not long after Eve herself. The ancient Greeks called them *godemiches,* the French, *bijoux indiscrets.* Made of glass or velvet, they were also known as *paprilla, cazzi, consolateurs,* and *bienfaiteurs.* Whatever one's position on the use of **mechanical devices** to achieve sexual fulfillment, we can agree that today's battery-powered vibrators are a vast improvement over 18th century ladies' penchant for turkey necks (headless, carcass-less turkey necks we pray, else it's a whole other story).

Today, if a woman employs an **indiscreet toy** too . . . enthusiastically upon herself, the medical community refers to it as a **picket fence injury.** Masturbatory mishaps by the male of the species seem to revolve around where, shall we say, the evidence might happen to land and is rarely lethal (notwithstanding Portnoy's worry about the bathroom light bulb). As far as we have evidence, that story about the young man whose investigation of the erotic effects of a vacuum cleaner hose left him with a severely elongated penis, is only an urban legend.

Although many believe that inflatable dolls are a recent phenomenon, we understand that there was such a thing for horny sailors called a **Dutch sea wife.** How anatomically correct these dolls were remains unascertained, but a **Dutch husband** was a **bed bolster.**

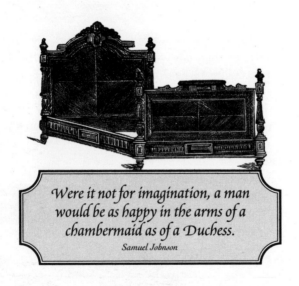

Were it not for imagination, a man would be as happy in the arms of a chambermaid as of a Duchess.

Samuel Johnson

Fleshly Treason

*What men call gallantry and the gods, adultery
Is much more common where the climate's sultry*

Lord Byron

Let us make this abundantly clear: **adultery** is what others commit. However, if one's own **shoes find themselves under another's bed,** one has suffered an **error of the blood.** A spouse's **infidelity** is grounds for divorce (if not an exchange of gunfire). If one **wanders** a bit ("I was thinking of you the whole time, honey"), it begs forgiveness.

In the 1900s, those guilty of **facile morals** committed a **marriage breach** by engaging in **illicit embraces.** Now, if

one's **affections stray,** it is called **offshore drilling, parallel parking,** or **extra curricular activity.** In any case, one is likely to be the recipient of a folded piece of paper announcing one's imminent **matchruptcy, dewife-ing,** or **splitting of the sheets** spelled **D-I-V-O-R-C-E** and the lawyers won't be kind. To remain faithful to one's vows, however, is to **keep league and truce.**

If one is not in a **committed relationship** and simply **screwing around,** it is an *affaire d' amour* (which is French for one night stand). Hence, one is in an **irregular situation, breaking the pale,** and **indecorously familiar.**

French does offer us very specific nuggets of circumlocutory gold. *Cinq-a-sept* refers to a customary afternoon period for quick **assignations,** hence the slang, *un petit cinq-a-sept* — a matinee; *Le demon de midi* — demon at noon: mid-life crisis or middle-aged men or women with eighteen-year-olds. (Ever notice that you never see someone living solely on social security sporting **arm candy**?)

Skin off old dead horses is to marry one's mistress.

> Q. How are a redneck divorce and a tornado alike?
> A. Somebody's gonna lose a trailer.

Of a man who was very unhappy in marriage and remarried immediately after his wife died, *Samuel Johnson* observed that it was "triumph of hope over experience."

Family Jewels
Baubles, Bangles and Beads

In polite company, they are **privates, urogenital concern, apparatus, loins,** or **vitals.** Indeed, sports announcers tend to identify this area as the **groin** or **lower abdomen,** apparently believing that to broadcast a more accurate "Ouch, that shot to the nuts had to hurt!" is not FCC-becoming.

In less discreet society, the **virilia** are called **doodads, marriage tackle, peculiar members, nads** (short for gonads), wares, **Adam's arsenal, stick and bangers,** *lingam* (from the Kama Sutra), **credentials, testimonials, pencil and tassels,** and **master of ceremonies.**

Whirleygigs, baubles, jinglebangers, whenneymegs, clangers, clappers, and **bangers** betray a great deal of fascination by the male of the species with their own apparatus. Regardless how noisy they all sound, none have, as far as is known, ever actually made any audible noise (not counting that poor man with testicular cancer whose doctor experimented by replacing his with ball-bearings — they didn't rust but his scrotum drooped abysmally).

Not unexpectedly, there is a specific term for the relaxation of scrotum — the **whiffles.** There is an equally curious name for the foreskin — **whickerbill.**

The Unruly Member (My Body's Captain)

There was a man from Ghent
Who had a penis so long it bent
It was so much trouble
That he kept it double
And instead of coming he went.

Only the **female pudendum** rivals the *membrum virile* for euphemistic grandiloquence such as **purple helmeted warrior of love.** Are *anthenaeum,* **Aaron's rod, carnal stump,**

Q. What did Adam say to Eve?

A. Stand back, I don't know how big this thing gets!

husbandman of nature, lance of love, man-root, torch of cupid, or **dribbling dart of love** too overwrought? May we suggest **swaydangle, larydoodle, tallywacker, flapper-prick,** or **bean-tosser** (a term of which one dares not guess a derivation). The basis for **bald-headed hermit** and **one-eyed trouser snake** seem far less obscure.

The ancient term for the male appendage was **yard.** This, mercifully, was when this word meant a stick or rod, not thirty-six inches. Almost as ancient is man's inclination to give his appendage a pet name. This selection often reflects the esteem (or lack thereof) in which said member is held by its owner — **Big Steve, Pile-Driver, merry-maker, General Custer, He Who Must Be Obeyed, Old Faithless,** or **Sleeping Beauty.** For pomposity, one cannot top **plenipo,** an abbreviation of plenipotentiary, which means "a diplomatic agent invested with full power to transact business." We also hear **Tommy, Dick, Harry, Willie, Giorgio, Percy,** and **Peter** (which reminds us that it was Groucho Marx who observed that actor Peter O'Toole's name was a penis euphemism times two).

The terms **bayonet, bazooka, blade, brachmard, dagger, dirk, gun, sword,** and **weapon** reflect the already acknowledged phallic/weapon imagery.

One can, of course, always call it **a penis.**

The Upright Wink

or *The little man and his boat*

Once described by some wit as the **factotum** (that which
controls all things), "it" is also **demesnes** (female domain).
If one cannot bring oneself to say the word **vagina,** try
hypogastric cranny (which will serve the purpose, no

doubt, of completely bewildering one's audience). More easily interpreted, if not particularly concise, we have *yoni, love's sweet quiver, delta of Venus, tufted love mound, Alter of Hymen, Adam's own* (beg pardon?), **nonny-nonny,** the **Ace of Spades** (clearly presaged the advent of Nair) and **the cabbage garden** (which does explain that inane story about where babies came from).

There once was a woman from China,
Who went to sea on a liner,
She slipped on the deck,
And twisted her neck,
And now can see up her vagina.

The **mons veneris** has generated a whole school of hirsute appellations, namely: **bearded clam, bearskin, brush brakes, bush, belly whiskers, thicket, down, nature's veil, fleece, fluff, motte,** and **beaver** (which alone accounts for the derivations **beaver-den, beaver-flick, beaver hunt, beaver pose, beaver-retriever,** and the ever-popular **beaver-shot**). The entire range of **pussy** metaphors would require corresponding redundancy and offers no particular revelations apart from the clearly onomapoetic term **kweef** which can most briefly be described as a **pussy-fart.**

There was a young lady named Brent
With a cunt of enormous extent
And so deep and so wide
The acoustics inside
Were so good you could hear when you spent

There is a rather indiscreet tale of a man who claims to have encountered a vaginal cleft so commodious that upon intromission he discovered "another bugger looking for his hat."

Nature's fonts

I once knew two sisters whose breasts
They exposed to their thunderstruck guests
A policeman was called
And the young chap, enthralled
Ogled, but made no arrests.

The female breasts. Or **appurtenances, bosom, bust, front, mammary glands, mammilla, teats, balcony, big brown eyes, headlights, lung warts, love bubbles, baloobas, bazookas, bazoongies, garbonzas, gazongas, kajoobies, toraborahs, maracas, lollies, diddies,** or **bodacious ta-tas** often encased in an **over-the-shoulder-boulder-holder** or **flopper stopper.**

Wasn't it one of the "friends" on TV who observed that it was God's plan that men didn't have **boobs** because, if they did, "they'd never get anything done"?

> I knew a young lady named Claire,
> Who possessed a magnificent pair,
> Or that's what I thought,
> Till I saw one caught,
> On a thorn and begin losing air.

Daft, mentally strange, barmy, unzipped, batty, berserk, insane, bonkers, cracked, loony, crazed, cuckoo, demented, deranged, peculiar, erratic, flaky, fruity, idiotic, insane, lunatic, mad, maniacal, nuts, potty, psycho, touched, unbalanced, unglued, unhinged, wacky

The Gazelles are in the Garden

They say that the difference between genius and stupidity is that genius has its limits.

Cerebrally Challenged

As spoken by a Texan, it is not "ig-nor-ant," but "ig-nernt," thus altering the meaning from "unlearned" to "too stupid to live." Our exploration of euphemisms for ignorance will be specific to the second definition.

Stupidity is the deliberate cultivation of ignorance.
William Gaddis

Obtuse, dull, imperceptive, opaque, stolid, unintelligent —in other words, a **peckerhead,** one whose **intellect is rivaled only by garden tools, got off the Clue Bus a couple**

of stops early, **is dumber than a box of hair** and **couldn't pour water out of a boot with instructions on the heel.**

The **cerebrally challenged** can occasionally be identified by physical characteristics: **narrow between the eyes, green as a gourd, room temperature IQ, wanting in the upper story, more nostril hair than sense, numb nuts, mouth-breather,** and **flat Peter** (trampled penis syndrome).

Statistics say that one out of every four Americans suffers from some form of mental illness. If your three best friends look okay, then it's you.

If one has **too much yardage between the goal posts,** one
is likely **smart as bait, not the sharpest tool in the shed,
the brightest crayon in the box,** nor **shiniest bulb on the
Christmas tree.** If one is **as fat as a hen in the forehead**
one is **in want of understanding, thick as a plank, dense
as a post, dumber than a bag of hammers, experiencing a
leak in the think-tank,** or **suffering a crop failure** and is
definitely **officer material.**

Whiff of the March Hare

Insanity doesn't only run in my family, it actually gallops.
Anon.

Non Compos Mentis

Although **lunatic** is a perfectly good word to describe
someone who is **absolutely crackers,** this loss of reason is
rarely addressed head-on. Circumlocution often implies the

afflicted **is not properly wound,** as in **wandered, un-hinged,** or **unglued.**

When someone is **dotty,** it is not unusual to allude to something lacking; therefore they are —

A few bricks shy of a load.
Couple of bubbles off plumb.
Several fries short of a happy meal.
One midget shy of a Fellini movie.
Two clowns short of a circus.
One Fruit Loop shy of a full bowl.
One taco short of a combination plate.
A few feathers short of a whole duck.
A few beers shy of a six-pack.
A few peas short of a casserole.

Or:

Both oars aren't in the water.
Only 50 cards in the deck.
Wants for some pence in the shilling.
Cheese slid off one's cracker.
All one's dogs aren't barking.
One's elevator doesn't go all the way to the top.
Lights are on but no one is at home.
No seeds in the pumpkin.
Doesn't have all his cornflakes in one box.
The wheel's spinning, but the hamster's dead.
Her sewing machine's out of thread.
His antenna doesn't pick up all the channels.
His belt doesn't go through all the loops.
Missing a few buttons on the remote control.

No grain in the silo.
Receiver is off the hook.
All foam, no root beer.

A Stranger to Reason

If absolutely nuts, one is **playing with the squirrels,** has **walnut storage disease,** or is **several nuts short of a full pouch.** In the pinball game of life, if one's **flippers are a little further apart than most,** one is **dicked in the nob, blinky** (milk about to sour), **off one's napper, has a slate loose,** is **damp in the attic,** one's **slinky is in a kink,** one's **skylight leaks,** or one's **drawers are left open.**

Of course, if one is wealthy anything queer one says or does is merely **eccentric.**

CAUTION
Even a fool can be right
once in a while.

'N What?

Or

Ode to Dan Rather

Lower'n the rent on a burning building
Jumpier'n virgin at a prison rodeo
Emptier'n a eunuch's underpants
Colder'n a well digger's ass
Stiffer'n a preacher's prick at a wedding
Tighter'n the bark on a tree
Smoother'n snot on a doorknob
Happier'n a coon on an ear of corn
Awkward'n a cow on skates
Lower'n a snake's belly
Slicker'n owl shit
Clumsier'n a pig on ice
Smaller'n a bar of soap after a hard day's wash
Colder'n a copper toilet seat in the Klondike
Deafer'n an adder
Fuller'n a tick
Hotter'n a fresh fucked fox in a forest fire

demented, deranged, peculiar, erratic, flaky, fruit

Happier'n a man who spent the day sorting
    out his concubine collection
Sicker'n a pizzened pup
Finer'n bee's wings
Noisier'n skeletons fucking on a tin roof
Uselesser'n pantyhose on a pig
Panickier'n a pig in a packing plant
Jittery'n than a long-tailed cat in a room
    full of rockers
Grinnin' like a possum eatin' cactus
Happier'n a baby in barrel of tits
Busier'n a dildo in a harem
Icier'n the shady side of a banker's heart
Madder'n a wet hen
Slowr'n a wet week
Happier'n clams in high water
Happier'n a puppy with two peters

The author acknowledges the Dover Publications Pictorial Archive series, and the satirical graphics of Cruikshank, Gillray, Hogarth, and Rowlandson.